PROJECTS ABOUT
Westward Expansion

Marian Broida

BENCHMARK BOOKS

MARSHALL CAVENDISH
NEW YORK

Acknowledgments

Thanks to the following individuals and groups for their assistance: Todd Arrington, historian, and Christy Sweet, museum technician, Homestead National Monument of America, Beatrice, Nebraska; Sandra Lowry, librarian, Fort Laramie National Historic Site; Ione Quigley, cultural resource management specialist, Sinte Gleska University; University of Washington Herbarium; Beverly and Arnold Slatin, and Shaina Andres, Beatrice Misher, and the View Ridge Boys and Girls Club, for testing activities.

Benchmark Books
Marshall Cavendish
99 White Plains Road
Tarrytown, NY 10591-9001
www.marshallcavendish.com

Text copyright © 2004 by Marshall Cavendish Corporation
Illustrations © 2004 by Marshall Cavendish Corporation

Library of Congress Cataloging-in-Publication Data

Broida, Marian.
        Projects about Westward Expansion / by Marian Broida.
              v. cm. – (Hands-on history)
Includes bibliographical references and index.
Contents: Introduction – The early frontier – The Oregon Trail –
Homesteading on the prairie.
        ISBN 0-7614-1604-8
Frontier and pioneer life—United States—Study and t
    teaching—Activity programs—Juvenile literature. 2. Frontier and
    pioneer life—West (U.S.)—Study and teaching—Activity
    programs—Juvenile literature. 3. United States—Territorial
    expansion—Study and teaching—Activity programs—Juvenile literature.
    4. West (U.S.)—History—Study and teaching—Activity
    programs—Juvenile literature. [1. Frontier and pioneer life. 2. United
    States—Territorial expansion. 3. West (U.S.)—History. 4. Handicraft.]
        I. Title. II. Series.
E179.5.B88 2004
979.5'03—dc21
        2003001934

Illustrations and maps by Rodica Prato

Historical Picture Archive/Corbis: 12. *Hulton/Archive by Getty Images:* 1, 19. *Nebraska State Historical Society:* 36. *North Wind Picture Archives:* 4, 7, 16, 20, 24, 32, 35, 42,

Printed in China

1 3 5 6 4 2

Contents

❧

Log cabins provided sturdy shelter and could be built quickly from materials available in the wilderness.

1

Introduction

❧

Do you smell corn cake baking by a fire? You are in a Kentucky log cabin in Daniel Boone's time.

Do you feel hard-packed dirt through the holes in your shoes? You are trudging beside a **covered wagon** along the Oregon Trail.

In this book you will travel along with thousands of Americans as they move west. As Americans settled the **continent** the **frontier** moved with them. You will travel first to Kentucky, part of the earliest frontier, in the year 1788. You will make the hard journey on the Oregon Trail around 1850. Finally, you will visit **homesteads** in Nebraska in the year 1885.

On your visits you will work and play as youngsters did in the past. You will weave a basket, stitch a **quilt** square, build a model covered wagon, and make a small blackboard, called a slate.

The settlers who moved west had courage. Often they were moving from cities to places with few comforts. They made their own clothes, houses, furniture, and food. Everyone, including the children, worked from dawn to dusk nearly every day.

Join the **pioneers**, and try your hand at history!

Daniel Boone opened up a trail from Virginia into "Kentucke." Called the Wilderness Road, it snaked across the Appalachian Mountains through a place called the Cumberland Gap. In time, the trail lengthened at both ends.

2
The Early Frontier

Americans were moving west before the country declared independence from England. In 1775, Daniel Boone led pioneers across the Appalachian Mountains into Kentucky. Soon settlers were pouring into the territories of Tennessee and Ohio, and then into Illinois, Michigan, Indiana, and Wisconsin.

Before the settlers arrived, these lands had been home to many different American Indian tribes, such as the Cherokee and Shawnee. The United States government forced the Indians out so the settlers could move in.

By 1840 most of these lands had become states. The frontier had moved west to California and Oregon.

Daniel Boone spent most of his life exploring and settling the American frontier. In this illustration he is seeing Kentucky for the first time.

Berry Basket

You are picking blackberries in the woods. Last night you finished weaving your berry basket out of thin strips of oak.

Suddenly you hear rustling, and you turn. A bear is lumbering toward the berry bushes. In a minute it will see you.

Clutching the basket, you tiptoe away—then run as fast as you can. "Ma! There's a bear in the woods!" you holler as you near the house. "Run, fetch Pa," she yells back. "And tell him to bring the gun!"

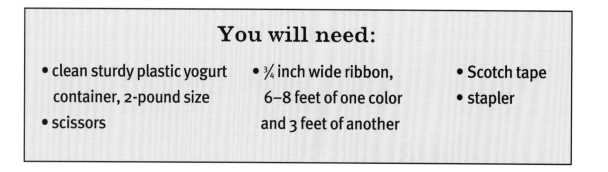

You will need:

- clean sturdy plastic yogurt container, 2-pound size
- scissors
- ¾ inch wide ribbon, 6–8 feet of one color and 3 feet of another
- Scotch tape
- stapler

1. Cut an even number of slits (twelve, fourteen, or sixteen) in the container, from top to bottom, about ¾ inch apart. Plan your last few slits when you have about 2 inches left. Leave the bottom whole.

2. Cut the longer ribbon in half. Tape one end to the outside of the container between two slits, near the bottom. Pull the ribbon inside through one of these two slits. Weave the ribbon in and out of the slits, as shown. Go all around the bottom. Each time you weave in or out, push the ribbon all the way down to the base of the container.

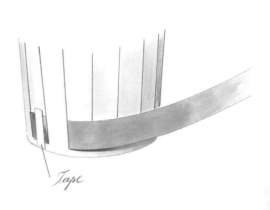

Tape

3. After circling the basket once, weave just above this first row. Go under the plastic strips you went over the first time, and over the strips you went under.

4. Keep weaving up to the top. When your ribbon runs out, staple the next piece (same color) to its end.

5. When there is no more room on the container for weaving, staple the ribbon to it, all around the top. Pull the end of the ribbon to the inside of your basket and trim.

6. Make a handle. Skipping the top loop, which is stapled to the container, push the second, different colored, ribbon straight down the outside of the basket, sliding under all the outer ribbon loops.

7. Pull the ribbon down under the bottom of the container. Slide the ribbon up the other side, going under the outer ribbon loops. Pull it over the top, leaving a comfortable handle.

8. Tuck the ribbon back under the outer loops on the first side so you have a double-thickness of ribbon for the handle.

Staple [ ] *Staple*

9. Staple the two ribbon layers together near one side of the container.

10. Pick up the basket by the handle. (This helps even out the ribbons.) Staple the handle to the top of the basket on each side.

11. Since you cannot wash your basket, put a clean plastic bag inside before you fill it with berries.

Blackberry Picking

Blackberries grow wild in many places. Pick them in late summer or early fall, just as pioneer children did.

1. Bring an adult along to help identify the blackberries. Be sure you can recognize blackberries. Avoid bushes that have been sprayed.

2. Look for the blackest, plumpest berries. Ripe berries come off easily. Overripe berries fall apart as you pick them.

3. To protect against thorns, it is best to wear a long-sleeved shirt and sturdy shoes. But you may still get a few pricks. Be careful.

4. Store your berries in the refrigerator, in a strainer on top of a plate. Rinse the berries just before eating. The pioneers ate blackberries plain, or baked into cobblers or pies.

Women sewed the top part of their quilts at home. They then attended social gatherings, called quilting bees, where everyone worked to sew the top to the stuffing and bottom layer.

Quilting

You are in bed with a fever. Nearby, your ma sits stitching scraps of cloth together to make a quilt. You see scraps from your old dress and your father's shirt.

"I want to make a little quilt," you whisper. You're afraid she will say you cannot sew well enough yet.

First Ma frowns. Then she says, "Why ever not? It might keep you busy until you get better."

You will need:

- two 8-inch square pieces of fabric. Cut-up cotton clothing is fine, with an adult's permission. Do not use bed sheets. They are difficult to work with.
- one 8-inch square piece of cotton or polyester batting for stuffing. If you cannot find batting, you can use a square of flannel.
- scissors
- 8 straight or safety pins
- needle
- thread
- large-eyed needle
- yarn or embroidery thread

You can hang your finished quilt square on the wall or use as a doll's blanket or a mat for a toy animal.

1. Choose one piece of fabric for the front, and one for the backing.

2. Place the stuffing on your work surface. Place the backing on top of the stuffing, right side up. On top of that, place the front, upside down, as shown. If the layers are different sizes, trim them so they are all the same size.

3. Pin through all three layers, near each edge.

4. Thread the needle and tie the two thread ends together, as shown.

5. Starting at one corner, stitch up and down through all three layers. Take small stitches. Stop when you have 3 to 4 inches of thread left.

6. Take three stitches backward over the part you sewed. Go up and down once for each stitch. These are called back stitches. Cut off the needle.

7. Thread the needle with a new piece of thread and tie a new knot. Sew until you have finished three sides. Make three backstitches each time your thread is about to end.

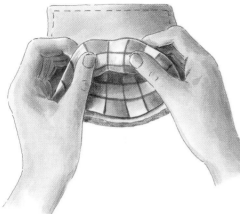

8. Remove all the pins. Slide your thumbs between the two layers of cloth on the unstitched end. Turn the square inside out, including the corners. Now there will be a piece of fabric on the front and another on the back, with stuffing in between.

9. Stitch along the last side. End with three backstitches.

10. Finish with a tie, like this: thread the large needle with an 8-inch piece of yarn or embroidery thread. Do not make a knot at the end.

11. Poke the needle through the quilt square's middle, front to back.

12. Pull one end of the thread through slowly, leaving a few inches of thread hanging out the front. Now, just ¼ to ½ inch away, poke the needle through the other way—back to front. With one hand, hang on to the end you left hanging out of the front while you pull the thread through with the other hand. You should end up with two tails in front.

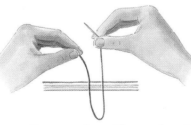

13. Remove the needle. Tie the tails together like a shoelace. Make a double knot. Trim the ends.

Johnnycake

Your parents were away when a snowstorm blew in. You and the younger children have been alone for three days. The youngest is crying.

"Hush," you say. "I'll make us some johnnycake."

You try to remember how Ma does it. You heat milk over the fire and add cornmeal. There is no salt left to put in.

The dough is baking by the fire when Ma opens the door.

"I smell johnnycake," she says, smiling. "However did you learn to make that?"

"I watched you do it," you say.

All cooking was done outdoors until a home was built.

You will need:

- oven
- 3-quart saucepan
- wooden spoon
- pot holders
- large bowl
- glass or metal pie pan, or large cast-iron frying pan
- timer
- table knife
- ⅔ cup milk
- 1 tablespoon butter, oil
- 2 cups cornmeal

Optional: ½ teaspoon salt, more butter, maple syrup or honey

1. Ask an adult to help. Pioneer children often got burned.

2. Preheat the oven to 350 degrees Fahrenheit.

3. Heat the milk in the saucepan on the stove, stirring often. Turn off the heat when the milk begins to steam.

4. Using a pot holder, pour the milk into the bowl. Carefully mix in the cornmeal.

5. If you have salt, mix it in.

6. Grease the pan with the butter or oil. Spoon on the dough. Shape it into one flat circle.

7. Using pot holders, put the pan in the oven.

8. Bake for twenty minutes. Check to see if the cake's edges are brown. If not, bake it five or ten minutes longer.

9. Take out the pan with pot holders. When it cools, cut the johnnycake into wedges, like pizza. Serve it with butter, maple syrup, or honey.

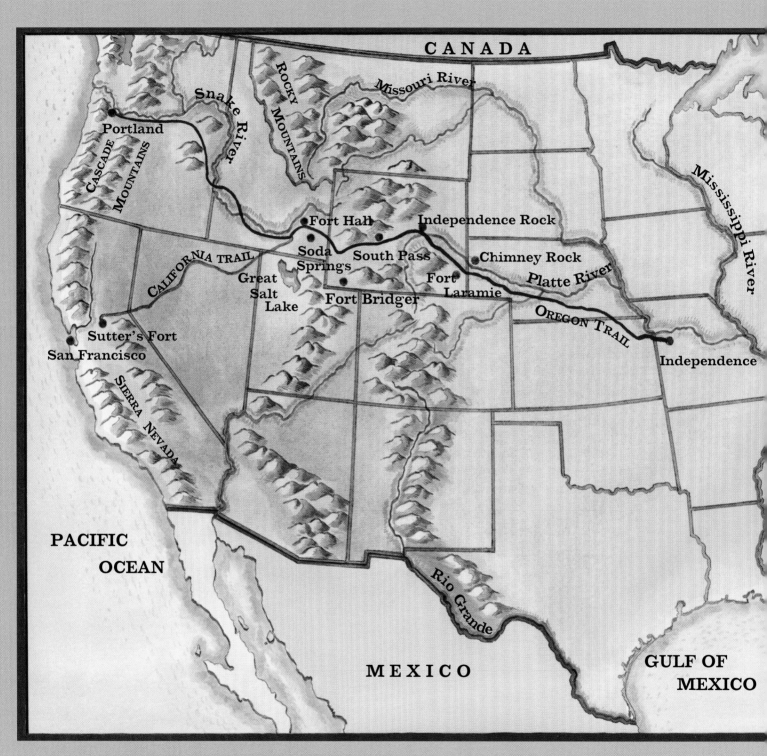

From 1843 to 1860 wagon train after wagon train followed the Oregon Trail. Starting at the Missouri River, the trail led west and north to Oregon. Many people took the trail over the Rocky Mountains, then branched off to California.

3

The Oregon Trail

Why would anyone cross the country in a covered wagon? People who did faced constant danger. Some drowned crossing rivers without bridges. Many died from illness. Some got lost and had to eat the **oxen** that pulled their wagons. Often they would starve anyway. Yet hundreds of thousands of people did travel west, walking beside covered wagons loaded with their things. They came seeking cheap farmland, adventure, or gold.

A wagon train moves west across the plains.

Covered Wagon

A covered wagon on the historic Oregon Trail in Scott's Bluff, Nebraska.

You and your family have just arrived in Independence, Missouri. Tomorrow you begin your six-month journey on the Oregon Trail. You will travel in a **wagon train** with many others.

Today you are helping your father paint OREGON OR BUST! on the wagon cover.

"Papa, what does this mean?" you ask him as you paint a letter.

"It means either we reach Oregon or we may die," he says. He is not smiling.

You swallow hard. All of a sudden you feel just a tiny bit scared.

You will need:

- scissors
- shoe box without lid
- pen or pencil
- 4 plastic lids from margarine or yogurt tubs (1- to 2-pound size)
- paper, 8 ½ by 11 inches
- markers
- glue stick
- large nail
- ruler
- 2 chopsticks or dowels, 4-6 inches longer than the shoe box is wide
- duct tape
- 4 strips of corrugated cardboard, 1 inch wide and 3 times longer than the box is wide
- piece of muslin fabric or an old sheet, cut to 2 inches longer than shoe box and 2½ times as wide
- Scotch tape

1. Cut a 2-inch-long slit along each corner at one end of the box.

2. Fold out the flap you cut, as shown, making a driver's seat.

3. Trace around each margarine lid onto the paper. Draw spokes, as shown, on the paper with a marker. Cut out the circles. Trim them, and glue them inside the lids.

4. Poke the nail through the middle of each wheel. Ask an adult for help.

5. Mark four dots—two on each long side of the box—for the wheels. Make each dot ½ inch from the bottom and 2 ½ inches from the end. Use a ruler. Poke the nail through each dot. Get help if you need it.

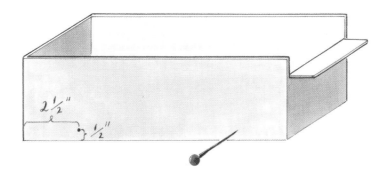

6. Slide the chopstick or dowel through the front of one wheel, the two holes in the box, and the back of another wheel. Wheel spokes should face out. Repeat at the other end of the box.

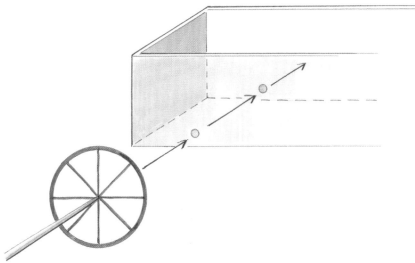

7. Wrap duct tape around the stick in front of each wheel, to help hold it on.

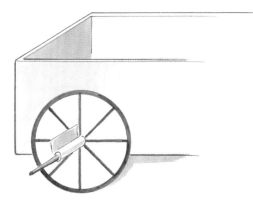

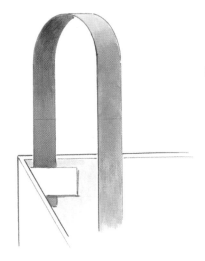

8. Bend a cardboard strip into an upside-down U. Use duct tape to attach one end to the inner side wall of the box, near the driver's seat. (Fasten it near the bottom of the box.) Attach the end to the opposite wall of the wagon, taping it to the inside.

9. Repeat with the other strips, putting one near each end.

10. Cover the hoops with the cloth. Trim the cloth if it is too big. Leave enough cloth so it can be folded under the first and last hoops.

11. You can write a phrase such as "Oregon or Bust!" on one side. First mark the area where you want the sign to be when it's on the wagon. Then take the cloth off to write on it.

12. Spread glue along the outside of each hoop. Replace the cloth with the writing on the outside. Press it on firmly. Let it sag a little between the hoops.

13. Fold the ends under the first and last hoops and tape in place.

The city of Deadwood, South Dakota, was founded in 1876 during the Black Hills gold rush.

Moccasins

Your father is a white man and a fur trader. Your mother is a Lakota Indian. You are with your father at a **trading post** along the Oregon Trail. Your father has come to trade furs and other things.

A man heading for Oregon in a wagon train wants to trade an iron pot for three pairs of moccasins. "Durn Indians," he grumbles to your father. "Rode all around the wagon train yesterday. Scared my wife and children near to death."

"Didn't hurt you none, did they?" says your father. "Probably my wife's people. She made those moccasins you're after."

The man grabs the moccasins and elbows his way out. You smile at your father.

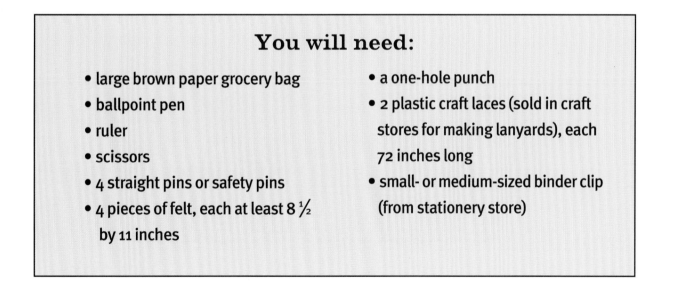

You will need:

- large brown paper grocery bag
- ballpoint pen
- ruler
- scissors
- 4 straight pins or safety pins
- 4 pieces of felt, each at least 8 ½ by 11 inches
- a one-hole punch
- 2 plastic craft laces (sold in craft stores for making lanyards), each 72 inches long
- small- or medium-sized binder clip (from stationery store)

1. Cut the bag open so it lies flat. Stand with your left bare foot in the middle of one blank side. Have a helper trace around your foot. Step off.

2. On the tracing that was just made, measure the distance from the middle of the heel to the tip of the longest toe.

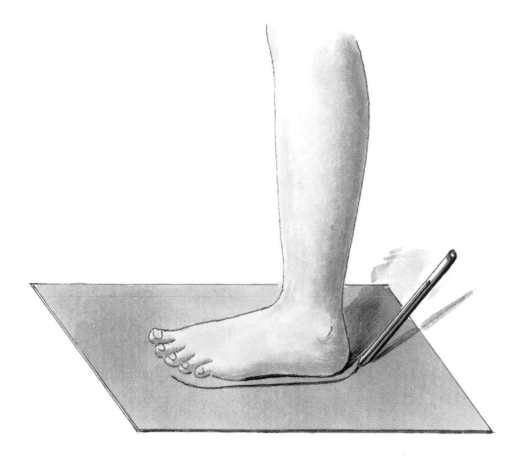

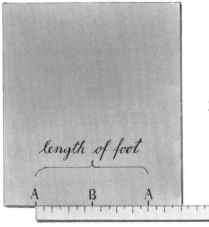

3. Copy this distance along the edge of another part of the bag as shown. Mark the two ends with little As. Measure and mark the center B.

length of foot

A   B   A

4. Using a ruler to measure the distance, mark dots 1/2 inch outside the foot tracing and 3/4 inch outside at the heel. Connect the dots, making a bigger shape.

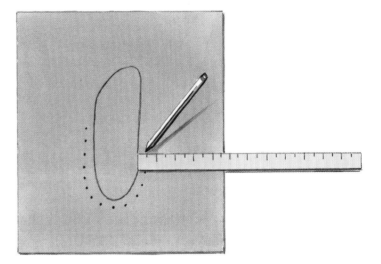

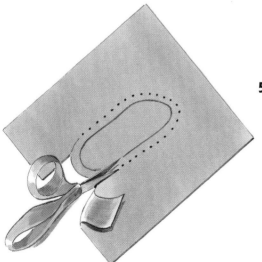

5. Cut out the bigger shape as shown. Mark it LEFT SOLE near the toe end.

6. Lay the cutout tracing against the line on the bag where you marked A and B, with the middle of the heel at the B. See illustration.

7. Mark a C on the bag, not on the cutout piece, at the tip of the longest toe.

8. Draw a smooth curve from the C to each A. The two curves will be a little different from each other. Take off the sole.

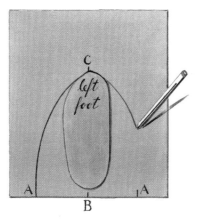

9. Make a dot 1 inch to the left of the B and mark it D. Rule a straight line from the D halfway up the drawing. Make another dot 1 inch to the right of the B, and make another line halfway up the drawing. Cut along each of these lines, starting with D and ending halfway up the drawing. Then cut out the whole shape. Mark it LEFT UPPER.

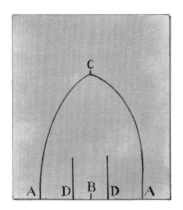

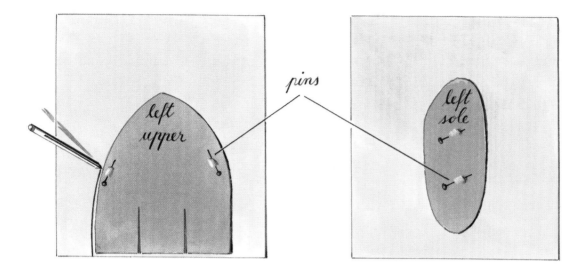

10. Pin the paper marked left sole and the one marked left upper each to its own piece of felt. Trace around them with the pen, including the two straight lines on the left upper. Unpin the felt and cut out the shapes. (Cut slits along the two straight lines on the upper.) Save the paper patterns.

11. Punch holes first around the felt sole and then around the upper ½ to ¾ inch apart, about ¼ inch from the edge, as shown. Punch no holes in the middle flap of the upper. Make sure there is a hole at each tip (the end of the longest toe).

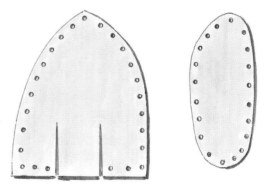